W9-APT-607

The International Design Library ®

American Rowhouse Classic Designs

Jonathon Scott Fuqua

Stemmer House
PUBLISHERS, INC.

Introduction

In America, the rowhouse is the dominant form of residential, urban architecture. From Charleston to Boston, it has functioned for 300 years, providing shelter for individuals of all socio-economic classes, from immigrant factory workers to robber barons. Successful rows, no matter their grandeur, have a rhythmic uniformity that, depending on the style, is often accentuated by subtle, spectacular or even dissonant variations among individual dwellings. Somehow, in a simple line of connected houses, where all except the end units are constrained by walls on two sides, architects and builders have created masterpieces of expression and form. Across America, rowhomes ride the varying topography of the country's earliest, most successful communities. The oldest and grandest examples—not necessarily synonymous—usually exist downtown, within the confines of the original city. From that point, huge deviations in style and type spread outwards, towards and sometimes into suburbia. What I have sought to examine in this book are the more classical structures, rowhomes built before World War II, to reveal them for what they are, symphonies and passages of beautiful art.

In no way have I attempted to create a definitive collection of American rowhouse types, for that would take volumes. Instead, I have tried to introduce distinctive periods and unique styles in order to help people see detail and design that are often overlooked. Sadly, America's western cities go unexamined (possible fodder for another book). For this book, I concentrated on the East Coast.

The rowhouse was carried to America in the hearts and minds of individuals emigrating from Europe, where for thousands of years residential dwellings have been built attached in rows. An examination of maps of ancient Rome reveal block upon block of connected homes. Later, middle-class contiguous houses occupied Renaissance villages, as well as the seafaring hamlets and cities through which immigrants later passed on their way to America.

Since the term for two adjoined dwellings is "duplex," and a freestanding house is a "single family home," I have defined the rowhome, or the townhouse (which is what anxious real-estate agents like to call them in an attempt to heighten their appeal), as one of a series of at least three connected residences. A row can cover an entire block, or, if it is small, as little as 900 square feet of space.

There are numerous reasons why rowhomes have been so popular in American cities, the least of which, I believe, is the myth that erecting against an already-existing dwelling was less expensive than constructing a four-walled building. Connecting houses created many complications, especially if they were built at different times by different individuals. One difficulty was engineering. Erecting against a preexisting house, especially on steep slopes or in loose soil, often presented quandaries. Digging out cellars or foundations against a structure can cause a collapse. Then there was the aesthetic problem (frequently overcome, but sometimes painfully disregarded). Visually connecting two diverse rowhouse types could destroy or augment a row. This opened a flood of subjective issues. However, when developers chose to disregard the aesthetic of a block, they often found their properties difficult to sell. Who would choose to live on a graceless street?

It could be said that greed, more than anything else, produced America's urban rowhouse communities. In growing cities, land became expensive; developers calculated their costs and quickly concluded that the more homes they could squeeze onto a block, the more money they'd make. In some cities, like Baltimore, municipal laws played a role as well. Cash-strapped customers were induced into the market with "ground rent," which allowed developers to sell their product inexpensively, because they maintained ownership of the parcel of land upon which they had built. The buyer then rented the land that his house occupied from the developer, perpetuating the desire to squeeze more and more homes onto less and less space.

If greed fueled rowhouse construction, then competition also spurred a rare combination of quality and public benevolence. Marketing among developers was fierce, and many depended upon their good reputation—as well as the beauty and quality of their product—to ignite customer interest. Even rowhomes designed for the working-class were affected by the competition within a city. Developers strove to bury their rivals with unparalleled amenities on the inside and high quality, stylish facades on the outside. This is why so many rows remain. For the most part, they are durable structures, made of quality materials, most of which would be too expensive to use today. (Strangely, the backs of rowhomes are often neglected mishmashes of inferior materials, jutting rooms and deep breezeways that allow light and air to penetrate into the back parlors and bedrooms. They were built as if no one would ever see them. And why not? Customers didn't seem to mind).

In regards to public benevolence, rowhouse entrepreneurs often saw the value in donating parks or squares to the city, then building up around them, shrewdly increasing the value of adjacent rows as well as those under construction nearby. This type of altruism bestowed good repute upon a developer while simultaneously increasing the worth of his portfolio. Donating property to the community was smart business. Even so, it should be noted that the squares and parks given to municipalities were and are some of the most beautiful public spaces in urban America.

Another simple reason for the success of rowhomes was standardization. As the Industrial Revolution jolted into high gear, developers were able to purchase huge lots of identical wooden columns, brackets and pressed tin (or zinc) cornices, spun and stamped in mass quantities by new machines. Local companies specialized in certain architectural elements, supplying hundreds of thousands to the building trades. Obviously, in rowhouse development, identical fixtures were a huge boon, allowing for construction on a larger scale than ever before. Yet this standardization also brought about an explosion of odd styles and regional diversity. Local companies developed signature lines and looks specific to certain cities, like Washington DC's ubiquitous cast iron stairways *(plate 25)*.

Between the founding of America and the beginning of World War II, rowhouses were built in nearly every architectural style popular with the American public. However, there have always been needs specific to the rowhome, no matter the type, because of its layout. Since capturing as much outside light as possible was necessary to illuminate deep interiors, most have windows as large or larger than their front doors. Across the bottom of these often exists an ornate series of cast iron grates or banisters designed to shield the inside from curious eyes. Further, due to the flat, clonelike nature of rowhouses, many architects, starting around the mid-nineteenth century, attempted to create fashionable, striking facades by pushing outwards from the buildings' surface with stylistic elements too heavy and dramatic for most single family homes. Grand lintels, bay windows, ornate cornices and a dramatic or elegant front stairway became common. Color schemes, however, maintained the trendy hues of the day.

Typically, rowhouse interiors embraced ingenuity while maintaining a fairly consistent layout over the years. Despite the vertical arrangement, architects had to pack the narrow spaces with the same fixtures required in free-standing homes. Steps trace walls or twist tightly from floor to floor, broken by a series of square landings. Huge skylights and skylight shafts that penetrate through every floor of the home make up for a lack of windows. Rooms often progress one after the other and are odd in shape to allow for the confined lateral space as well as ventilation. Transom windows and high ceilings were a popular way to maintain air flow and create an openness to quarters deep in the house. Most rowhomes have long, narrow hallways that stretch from front to back like ice caves. In the Victorian era, many were built with a small, secondary stairwell for servants, as well as dumbwaiters that operated from the top floor to the basement, where, in the higher style homes, the kitchen was located.

Architecturally, I feel that New York has the most stunning examples of rowhouse design. The "brownstones," as they are called, are uncommonly diverse and usually very beautiful. The homes along Park Slope and Brooklyn Heights proclaim middle-class wealth, sophistication and good taste. Their brownstone veneer (actually red sandstone) visually connects them from block to block and creates a quality of light and shadow that cannot be matched by limestone, brick or wood. The rowhouses in Manhattan are usually a higher style (often Beaux Arts) with fashionable limestone finishes, but they just don't have the same free-wheeling sense of design or overall feeling of community as those built for the middle (maybe upper-middle) class masses. For the most part, I would say this is common in every city. Except for rare examples, I tend to prefer the unpretentious, unexpected character of homes built for common people.

New York might have the most consistently beautiful rowhomes, but Baltimore is, without argument, the rowhouse capital of the East Coast. Countless ranks extend from block to block in all directions. The eras represented range from Federal Style, downtown, to Colonial Revival, on the outskirts of the city's limits. Baltimore has earned the title not simply because of sheer numbers but for the overwhelming diversity and creativity of the dwellings. After a subdued version of High Victorian Italianate ran its course, and designers dabbled with aspects of the French-inspired Second Empire Style, Baltimore architects and developers seemed to fall in love with every style, sometimes all at once. There are stunted versions of high-style rowhomes for the working class, and strange conglomerations of spindles, lintels, bricks, stones, stained glass and cornices for wealthier customers. Certain rows look as though the architect had lost his mind in the middle of drawing plans, and others are beautiful and unexpected masterpieces of No-Style and Every-Style. Driving through Baltimore's hundreds of human-scale rowhouse neighborhoods is an amazing experience.

Charleston should be cited for its Colonial and Federal Style rows, austere yet weathered and kindly. To get a faint idea of what living in a rowhouse was like as far back as 300 years ago, a visit is necessary. It is an amazing stroke of luck that these buildings remain after earthquakes, fires, hurricanes and a military siege during the Civil War. That they do can be credited to luck and a bout of economic dormancy. Without money, the city was unable to develop. Hence the old town remains.

Boston has a huge array of rowhouse types. Certain areas resemble Charleston, while others favor Philadelphia or New York. Throughout Boston's existence, it has been the influencer and the influencee, both inspiring and stealing from other East Coast cities. Today, it has diverse, livable rowhouse enclaves, from Back Bay to dazzlingly restored Beacon Hill. For that reason, it feels fully functional and fairly undiminished, when compared to cities like Baltimore.

Washington DC's rowhomes are unanticipated and gorgeous. Throughout the capital exists the full complement of styles, most influenced by a bizarre combination of Southern gentility and worldly awareness. Washington is packed with stunning examples of Federal Style and Victorian rowhomes. Nonetheless, the area I enjoy most is Dupont Circle, which is crowded with strange, eclectic rows, huge turn-of-the-century dwellings that don't have any discernible stylistic tendencies.

I mention Philadelphia last because in its earlier years it had an enormous, anchoring influence on Baltimore, Washington and even, possibly, Charleston. Also, Philadelphia has an elephantine range of housing types, approaching Baltimore in architectural oddities and numbers. I will never forget spotting a queer little row of working-class clapboard and brick Second-Empire-influenced homes, complete with mansard roofs and turrets (*plate 11*). You don't see those every day. And then there's Society Hill, with its austere, well-kept Federal Style showpieces (similar in some ways to Boston's Beacon Hill). On the whole, I believe that they form the most homogeneous late 18th-century urban setting still extant in America. If you can block out the parked cars, walking it can be an unforgettable sensation.

In the end, developers gave up on the rowhouse in response to public demand. By the turn of the 20th century, streetcars and trains began what the automobile and blockbusting would finish. The general public no longer had to live so close to their jobs, and in the wide open spaces outside of town, the single-family home overcame the rowhouse as the dwelling of choice. Then, after World War II, suburbia grew to be the symbol of white middle-class success. However, not everyone with the financial means chose to depart, although many felt pushed by their own prejudices or the very real fear that they would lose their life savings in cities where property values were plummeting. Today, the steep levels of decline have abated; however, the damage has been done. It will take sweeping reforms to curtail suburban sprawl and entice the middle-class back into America's cities.

When I walk through many rowhouse neighborhoods, I get the feeling that I'm strolling through the remains of a once great, now-lost civilization. I wonder if individuals from the Dark Ages felt similarly upon finding remnants of buildings from the defunct Roman Empire. It is sad that so many Americans have forgotten that at one point in our history, beauty and quality were as important as function. I fear that as the years go by, block upon block of our oldest, most important urban housing will fall to bulldozers and wrecking balls, all in a well-intentioned effort to update the ancient and (I admit) sometimes deteriorating housing stock of America's inner cities. The irony is that as the rows disappear, a Neo-Traditional movement is sweeping the country. Developers and planners now realize that what makes a community is interaction among its residents, and rowhouse dwellers, by condition, communicate. Suburbia, with its isolated houses and bare spaces, doesn't facilitate much contact. So now America's suburbs will begin to resemble its cities, except that they will be devoid of the architectural drama or graceful symphony created by the developers of the past. It seems shameful not to salvage the beauty that already exists.

Jonathon Scott Fuqua

Plates

1 Historic Charleston, Charleston, SC • early 1700s • Colonial Style with Caribbean and English Country House influences

2 Historic Charleston, Charleston, SC • late 1700s to early 1800s • Georgian Style

3 Society Hill, Philadelphia, PA • late 1700s to early 1800s • Federal Style

4 Historic Charleston, Charleston, SC • early 1800s • Federal Style in Charleston "single house" manner

5 Beacon Hill, Boston, MA • early to mid 1800s • Greek Revival Style

6 Charleston, Boston, MA • early to mid 1800s • Greek Revival Style

7 Georgetown, Washington, DC • mid 1800s • Early American Victorian with Aesthetic influences

8 Capital Hill, Washington, DC • mid 1800s • High Victorian in the Italianate Style

9 Historic Charleston, Charleston, SC • mid 1800s • Victorian Folk

10 Upper East Side, New York City, NY • mid to late 1800s • High Victorian in the Second Empire Style

11 West Philadelphia, Philadelphia, PA • mid to late 1800s • High Victorian in the Second Empire Style

12 Bolton Hill, Baltimore, MD • mid to late 1800s • High Victorian in the Italianate Style with Second Empire influences

13 Bolton Hill, Baltimore, MD • mid to late 1800s • High Victorian in the Italianate Style with Second Empire influences

14 Reservoir Hill, Baltimore, MD • mid to late 1800s • High Victorian in the Queen Anne Style with Eastlake and Stick Style influences

15 Bolton Hill, Baltimore, MD • mid to late 1800s • Victorian in the Queen Anne Style with Eastlake influences

16 Park Slope, New York City, NY • mid to late 1800s • Late Victorian in the Italianate Style

17 Park Slope, New York City, NY • mid late 1800s • Late Victorian in the Renaissance Style with Second Empire influences

18 Park Slope, New York City, NY • mid to late 1800s • Late Victorian Eclectic with Italianate and Second Empire influences

19 Brooklyn Heights, New York City, NY • mid to late 1800s • American Victorian

20 Mount Vernon, Baltimore, MD • mid to late 1800s • Late Victorian

21 Back Bay, Boston, MA • mid to late 1800s • Victorian in the Italianate Style

22 Society Hill, Philadelphia, PA • late 1800s • Late Victorian in the Richardsonian Romanesque Style

23 Dupont Circle, Washington, DC • late 1800s • Late Victorian in the Richardsonian Romanesque Style with Italian Renaissance elements

24 Capital Hill, Washington, DC • very late 1800s • Late Victorian in the Queen Anne Style

25 Capital Hill, Washington, DC • very late 1800s • Late Victorian in the Queen Anne Style

26 Capital Hill, Washington, DC • very late 1800s • Edwardian with Neo-Greek Revival and Second Empire influences

27 Charles Village, Baltimore, MD • very late 1800s • Edwardian with French Eclectic influences

28 Georgetown, Washington, DC • very late 1800s • Edwardian with French Eclectic and Italian Renaissance influences

29 Upper East Side, New York, NY • very late 1800s • Beaux Arts Style

30 Upper East Side, New York, NY • very late 1800s • Beaux Arts Style

31 Upper East Side, New York, NY • around 1900 • Beaux Arts Style

32 Dupont Circle, Washington, DC • around 1900 • Edwardian Eclectic with Italianate and French Eclectic influences

33 Georgetown, Washington, DC • very early 1900s • Edwardian Eclectic with Italianate and French Eclectic and Richardsonian Romanesque influences

34 Charles Village, Baltimore, MD • very early 1900s • Edwardian Eclectic with Mission and Italianate Style influences

35 University City, Philadelphia, PA • very early 1900s • Edwardian Eclectic with Italianate and Tudor Style influences

36 Hampden, Baltimore, MD • around 1900 • Vernacular swell front

37 Charles Village, Baltimore, MD • early 1900s • Edwardian Eclectic with Italianate, Neoclassical and Mission Style influences

38 Mayfield, Baltimore, MD • early 1900s • Edwardian Eclectic with Italianate and Neoclassical Style influences

39 Mayfield, Baltimore, MD • early 1900s • Edwardian with Neoclassical Style influences

40 Charles Village, Baltimore, MD • early 1900 • Edwardian Eclectic with English Country Home influences

41 Belair Edison, Baltimore, MD • early to mid 1900s • Eclectic Colonial Revival Style

42 Wyman Park, Baltimore, MD • early to mid 1900s • Colonial Revival Style

Bibliography

Buisseret, David, *Historic Architecture of the Caribbean.* Exeter, NH: Heinemann, 1980

Calloway, Stephen, and Elizabeth Cromley, *The Elements of Style.* New York: Simon and Schuster, 1991

Lockwood, Charles, *Bricks & Brownstones: the New York rowhouse, 1783-1929, an architectural and social history.* New York: McGraw-Hill, 1972

Marion, John Francis, *The Charleston Story: Scenes from a City's History.* Harrisburg: Stackpole Books, 1978

McAlester, Virginia and A.Lee McAlester, *A Field Guide to American Houses.* New York: Alfred A. Knopf, 1984

Poppeliers, John C., and Allen S. Chambers Jr., *What Style is it?: A Guide to American Architecture.* Washington, DC: Preservation Press, 1983

Rehbein, Leslie, and Kate E. Peterson, *Beyond the White Marble Steps: A Look at Baltimore Neighborhoods.* Baltimore: The Committee, 1979

Rifkind, Carole, *A Field Guide to American Architecture.* New York: New American Library, 1980

Scott, Pamela, and Antoinette J.Lee, *Buildings of the District of Columbia.* New York: Oxford University Press, 1993

Shivers, Natalie W., *Those Old Placid Rows: The Aesthetic and Development of the Baltimore Rowhouse.* Baltimore: Maclay and Associates, 1981

Smith, G.E. Kidder, *The Architecture of the United States.* Garden City: Anchor Press, 1981

Southworth, Michael, and Susan Southworth, *AIA Guide to Boston.* Chester: Globe Pequot Press, 1984

Waterman, Thomas Tileston, *The Dwellings of Colonial America.* Chapel Hill: University of North Carolina Press, 1950

Weeks, Christopher, *AIA Guide to Washington DC.* Baltimore: Johns Hopkins University Press, 3rd edn, 1994

Willensky, Elliot and Norval White, *AIA Guide to New York.* San Diego: Harcourt Brace Jovanovich, 3rd edn, 1988

2

13

15

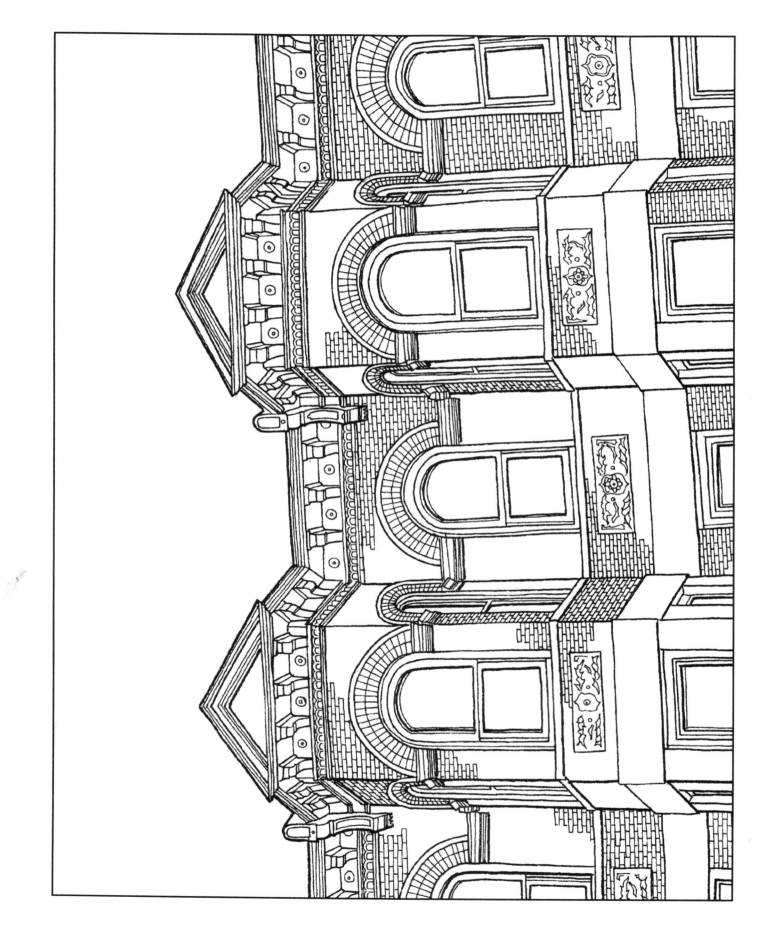

21

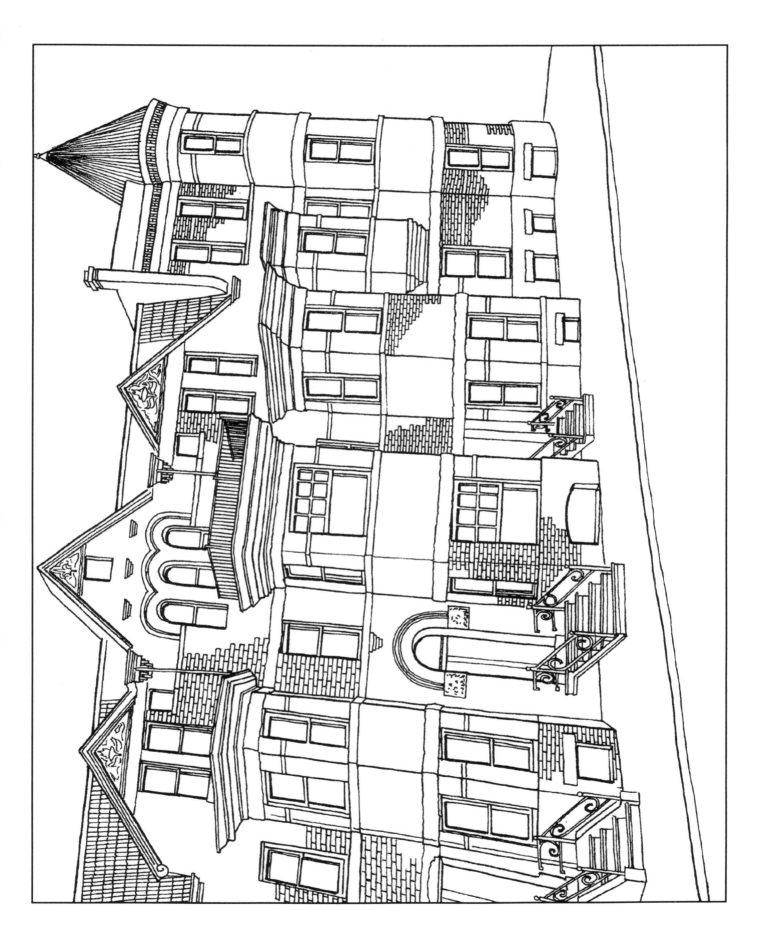

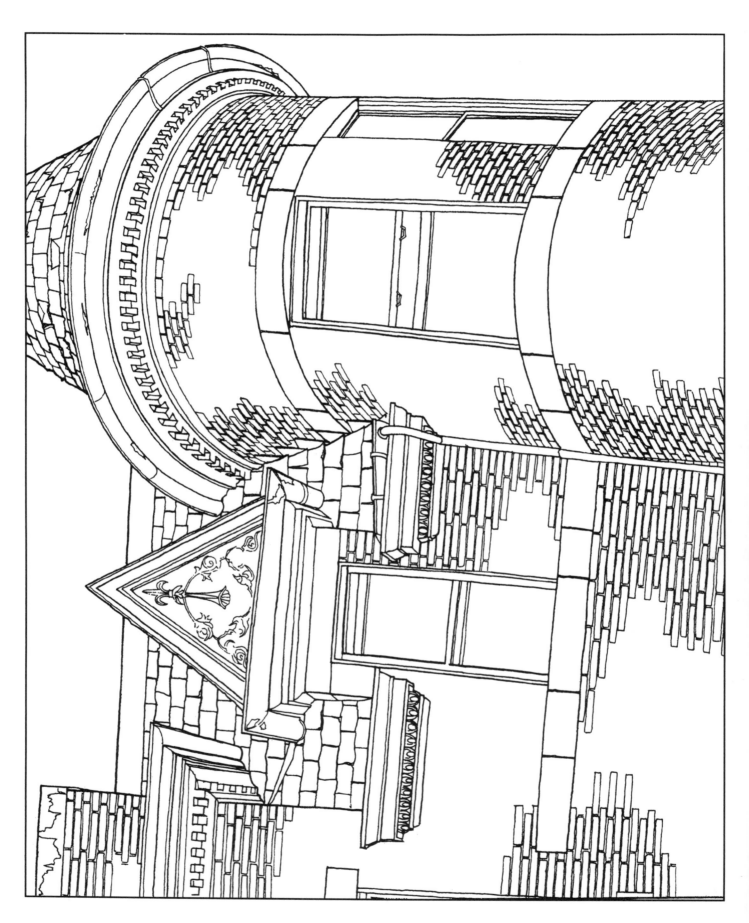

34

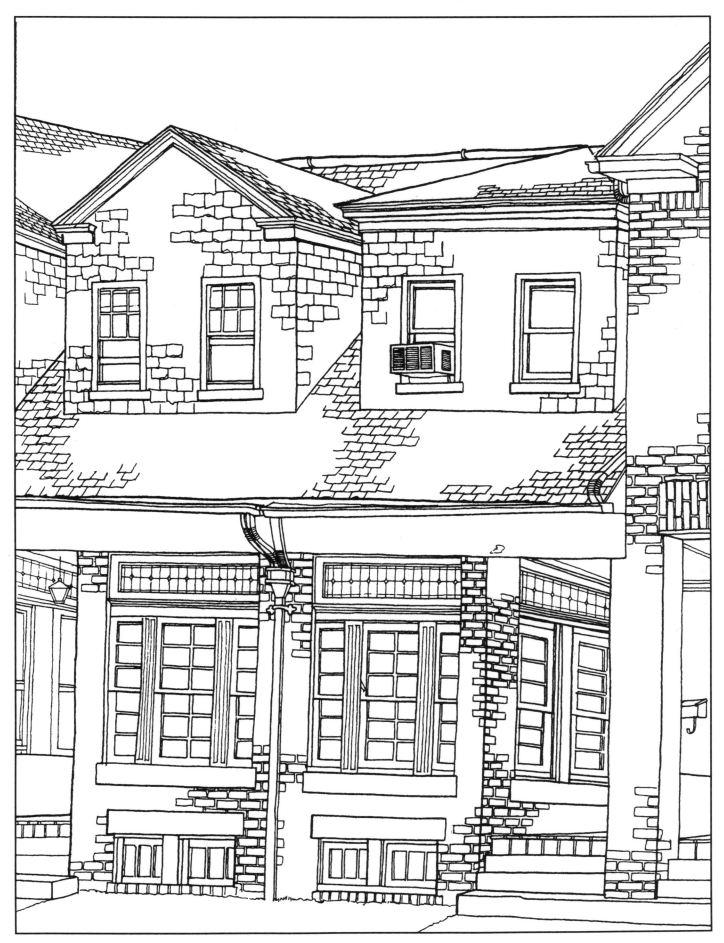

41

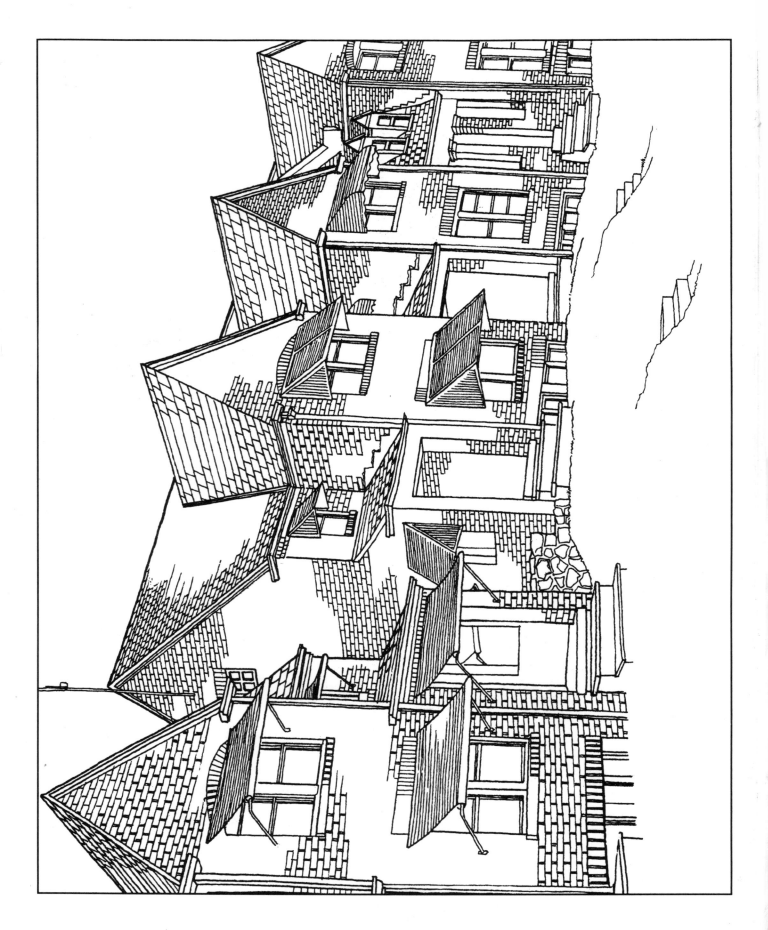